POEMS FROM A GRIEVING HEART

A Time for Hope after Losing a Spouse

Joanne Coleman

Copyright ©2025 by Joanne Coleman (Higher Ground Books & Media)
All rights reserved. No part of this publication may be reproduced in any form, stored in a retrieval system, or transmitted in any form, or by any means (electronic, mechanical, photocopying, recording or otherwise) without prior permission by the copyright owner and the publisher of this book.

Scripture taken from the HOLY BIBLE, NEW INTERNATIONAL VERSION®. NIV®. Copyright © 1973, 1978, 1984 by International Bible Society. Used by permission of Zondervan. All rights reserved worldwide.

Higher Ground Books & Media
Springfield, OH 45504
www.highergroundbooksandmedia.com
highergroundbooksandmedia@gmail.com

Because of the dynamic nature of the Internet, any web addresses or links contained in this book may have changed since publication and may no longer be valid. The views expressed in the work are solely those of the author and do not necessarily reflect the views of the publisher, and the publisher hereby disclaims any responsibility for them.

Any people depicted in stock imagery are being used for illustrative purposes only.

Printed in the United States of America 2025

Cover Design by: Leslie Shawn Fritz

DEDICATION

This book of heartfelt poems is dedicated to my late husband, Ronald Dean Coleman, who passed away unexpectedly in September of 2023. He was the most selfless man to grace my life. Everything I do is in his memory for I am now the memory keeper of his life.

This book is also dedicated to my six children and fifteen grandchildren who bless my life every day and remind me of the goodness of God.

FOREWORD

Walking alongside someone provides insight into their lives that you might not gain otherwise. I have had the incredible privilege of walking with Ron and Joanne Coleman through their pain, grief, and loss. Joanne has suffered since she lost her best friend, the love of her life, and her partner on this piece of rock we call Earth.

Ultimately, I stood before Joanne and the family at Ron's homegoing service. How do you put into words, or harder yet, in an hour, the impact that this man had in his home, with his kids, grandkids, the school he taught and coached, and the community that he loved?

To be human is to suffer. I don't know anyone that would disagree with that, and yet no one likes it! So how do we grieve, and in our grief, how can we express that to a world that knows suffering? Joanne has done just that. She has used the power of words and poetry to capture the pain and the joy. The strength that she has discovered through her God jumps off the page of each poem.

If you are suffering or have suffered and there is a lingering ache, you would do well to thumb through these pages. You would discover that you are not alone. There will be a sigh of relief and joy that trickles in, slowly turning into a raging river of hope.

I have personally had a front-row seat to Joanne's story of suffering that truthfully started before the loss of her soulmate. A story that culminates in this loss, yet the words cover a lifetime of pain. Joanne is the "poster child" of the truth that "to all who mourn, He will give a crown of beauty for ashes." (Isaiah 6:13)

Read away and find hope!

Dr. David Smith, pastor, and friend

INTRODUCTION

This book of poems is dedicated to my late husband, Ron Coleman, who passed away on September 21, 2023. Ron was a man of integrity, humility, selflessness, compassion, and kindness every day of his 72 years on this earth.

We often jokingly talked about who would "go first," and he would always tell me he wasn't going anywhere. God had other plans for Ron. He had multiple illnesses but didn't die from any of them. He was a survivor and conqueror in all his health problems. He came home from school on September 6, 2023, saying he was tired. He had a catastrophic stroke and subsequent brain bleed and passed 15 days later after futilely trying to participate in a therapy that was destined from the beginning to fail.

Ron was highly esteemed in the community as a teacher, coach, mentor, and administrator. He taught in multiple schools in the area and coached multiple sports in his almost forty-year teaching career. His last assignment at Stebbins High School enabled him to positively impact the students, teachers, staff, administrators, and schoolboard members to such a degree that they dedicated the renaming of their gymnasium to him. It is now called the Ron Coleman Gymnasium.

I was so proud of him every day of the 30 years we were together. He also impacted my life to such a degree that the

lessons I learned just from living with him are engraved in my heart forever.

I began writing these poems shortly after he died as a cathartic tool to help me grieve. Grief will never end. It doesn't have a time limit. The deeper the love, the deeper the grief. I have to learn to live with a heavy heart and still allow a part of my heart to propel me toward a new life without him. As I learned in the Griefshare program, I have to go through this because I loved.

My hope is that you will find some sense of comfort in the poems I have written from a raw and damaged heart. Yet, a heart filled with hope for a different future.

Author contact: jmpiccari120151@gmail.com

WITHOUT YOU

Another day dawns without your sweet smile, soft kiss goodbye when you go off to school, and charming morning text to see if I am all right.

Another day dawns without your love shadowing my day, without your concern about my safety, without the annoying kitchen door you locked behind you as a reminder of your protection.

Another afternoon creeps up without your all-encompassing energy talking about your beloved students, and another early evening slides into view without seeing you in the garden pruning the fruits of your labor.

Another night arrives without your arms around me, your hand caressing mine, your words a soft blanket of love and grace.

Another day went by without you...

WHEN…

When did you realize you were having a stroke?
When did you understand the profound effect, the stroke had on you?
When did you realize that you were never going to be whole again?
When did you understand the stark reality that I could not care for you?
When did you see that everything in our life together was changing and would never be the same?
When did you realize I would be alone for the rest of my life?
When did you visualize me carrying on without you?
When did you understand that our life together was coming to an end?
When you looked at me, what did you think at that moment?
When you sluggishly winked at me, what were you trying to convey?
When you looked at me that fateful last day and mouthed "I love you," what did you know?
When did you know you were slipping into a realm that was not my time in which to be?
When did you know you were looking at me for the last time?
When did you know I would now be alone?
When did you know….

GHOSTING GRIEF

I reach out in the dense darkness of night,

for the hand that I will never hold again.

I feel the desperate need for security your hand always provided me with.

I reluctantly dismiss the stinging tears trying to pour through the lids of my blind faith.

I am softly ghosting this grief because it is not comforting me.

IN ONE MONTH'S TIME

I awoke today with a heart too heavy to carry. It is a month today that marks you gone. It is still so surreal. Your frightening absence now in my life has created a lacuna of uncertainty and hopelessness. Some days, I am just okay- most days I am locked in the fugue of an ethereal bubble of sadness.

The days since your death go by so hauntingly slow, yet here we are at the month marker. My sense of self is all but devoid of logic. I am struggling with the concept of a future without you. You were the better half of us--the calm half, the patient half, the compassionate half, the loving half, and the selfless half.

Now I am trying to navigate my existence without those qualities to steer me daily. To say I miss you is a misnomer- -it is walking through my life without you now, finding out who I am without you now, living a yet-to-be-identified purpose without you now.

BITTERSWEET HOLIDAYS

The silence in this home is deafeningly loud without you in it. The holidays will be tough. We will be celebrating our wedding anniversary on Christmas Eve. I cannot even begin to consider participating in that day. Every year it was what we looked forward to, what we cherished as a family, honored what was most important to us-- our life together.

My birthday is December 1st, a day you treasured more than me. You made it so special for me. I cannot turn another year older without you here. It is just too much to bear... your absence resonates so loudly in my head, in my heart, and in my spirit. A spirit broken, a heart shattered with irreparable damage.

MY HERO

Everyone who met you benefitted from your boundless kindness and encompassing love. You had a way to make someone feel like they were the only person in the room, the only person you cared about....

Missing my hero every minute of every day. I promise to execute your legacy of kindness and selflessness...

You will always be my hero. You fought so many battles, most of them you would not share to protect me. I know you tried your best with this last battle, but I saw in your eyes the acknowledgment and reluctant acceptance that you could not go on like that.

Your courage has always inspired my soul and spirit. You showed me what resilience was all about in the most gracious selfless way. I am realizing more and more each day what a profound influence you had on my life, and our life together, and how precious that was to you. It is the endearing things I remember that hold me captive in the shadow of your stark absence. You will always be my hero.

THE FUTILE FIGHT

Never will I forget seeing you fight to want to live.

Never will I forget seeing you struggle to move your left side.

Never will I forget the flat affect I futilely tried to look through to see the real you.

Never will I forget the crippled wink in your eye when you helplessly looked at me.

Never will I forget the half smile you forged amid a stroke-induced asymmetry.

Never will I forget you saying I saved your life again.

Never will I forget the lost look in your eye as you faded into that lacuna of space between here and there.

Never will I forget the genuine and sacred love you gave me to the utmost degree.

Never will I forget how much you loved me.

I loved you too....

I AM FROM

I am from being half in a world of wholes.

I am from following in the footsteps of your life.

I am from grief that is magnified every day in its attempt to ambush me.

I am from tears that flow at the most unexpected times and drop onto the words that escape me.

I am from trying to fill the meaningless space your absence created.

I am from never sleeping on your side because it hurts too much.

I am from the sadness that permeates the air and stifles my already labored breath.

I am from remembering the selfless things you always did.

I am from a grateful heart that your life lessons are still teaching me to navigate my future roads.

I am from being your favored student in Study of Life 101.

I am from the haunting need to continue your mission of love and empathy, caring and kindness.

I am from long, dark, and lonely nights without your arms encircling me in protective custody.

I am from moments of celebrating the peace you now have at the expense of my security and immense loss.

I am from the tortuous bereavement of the loss of the love of my life.

I am from starting anew where you drifted into the arms of Christ.

I am from the enormous depth of love that I did not fully and wholly acknowledge until you left me.

I am from losing you...

THE IMPACT OF YOUR DEATH

The impact of your death has abruptly and forever changed my life.

The impact of your death has left me alone and afraid.

The impact of your death has me drifting in a sea of whys and what-ifs.

The impact of your death revealed that everything I knew about us was turned into a story instead of my life.

The impact of your death sees me constantly crying when someone speaks of how sorry they are that you are gone.

The impact of your death magnified the unparalleled influence you had on me and the abundance of love you had for me, which was overwhelming.

The impact of your death showed me the myriads of blessings you bestowed on everyone you met.

The impact of your death unleashed the lessons you taught me as pieces of precious epiphanies falling around me in a protective bubble of the character traits garnered through your life.

The impact of your death causes me to see you in all things in my life, which is both solacing and disturbing—a constant reminder of my days in your absence.

The impact of your death tore me in half, and I am now in the tortuous position of finding myself without you.

The impact of your death forces me to see a view of my future that is devoid of further joy.

The impact of your death puts me in the unenviable position of no longer being part of a couple.

The impact of your death secures my status as a widow. One cut in half through a cascade of tragic blessings.

WHAT I WOULD TELL YOU NOW…

I would tell you that you were the most precious gift to me.

I would tell you that I wished I had told you, "I love you" more.

I would tell you that you were such an extraordinarily kind and caring soul.

I would tell you that your smile I craved every day because it lit up my life.

I would tell you that the magnitude of the impact you had on so many people overwhelmed me.

I would tell you I wish we had renewed our wedding vows like you so wanted to do.

I would tell you that your unwavering love always encompassed me in a safe and protective cocoon.

I would tell you that my nights are very lonely and cold without you.

I would tell you that you have tattooed yourself on the fabric of my heart forever.

I would tell you that you were the most handsome man I have ever known.

I would tell you that your laugh was infectious beyond humanly possible.

I would tell you not to leave me alone like this.

I would tell you I am happy you are free of physical and mental suffering at the pervasive risk of my immense loss.

I would just tell you…. everything unsaid.

GRATITUDE

I am grateful for every hour that I spent with your love.

I am grateful for the family we created.

I am grateful for my children who continue to be there for me in all ways subtle and discernible.

I am grateful for the mercies God has bestowed on me despite my restless and rebellious ways.

I am grateful for the sounds of music that resonate through my soul and bring memories of you front and center.

I am grateful for the home, the haven that you worked so hard to provide me with.

I am grateful for this safe harbor in which I now reside alone.

I am grateful for your shadow looming large behind every footstep I now take.

I am grateful for the abundant and limitless love you wrapped me in for thirty years.

I am grateful for every holiday on which we celebrated all our numerous blessings.

I am grateful for the selfless way you lived your life even amid the many trials and tribulations you suffered.

I am grateful for your legacy, which I promise to carry on.

I am grateful for every single act of extraordinary kindness you freely and lovingly gave to all you met.

I am grateful for quiet moments that provide me with the solace of celebrating our lives together.

I am forever grateful for the one-in-a-million chance to be your wife, your lover, your friend, your confidante, and your heart.

I am just forever grateful for the you who spent thirty years with the me that loves you still…

IF I COULD GO BACK IN TIME

If I could go back in time, I would tell you I love you more than I did.
If I could go back in time, I would renew our vows to each other.
If I could go back in time, I would be more patient with you when you focused on everyone you met to a fault.
If I could go back in time, I would be more romantic and dance joyfully with you every day to the music of our hearts.
If I could go back in time, I would spend time engaging in the things you loved, maybe even football.
If I could go back in time, I would kiss you more, because your lips have always enchanted me.
If I could go back in time, I would never put off intimacy with you just because I was too tired.
If I could go back in time, I would curl up in your great protective wings and stay there for more than a minute.
If I could go back in time, I would explore experiences with you through the traveling you always wanted to do.
If I could go back in time, I would lay down my life for you.
If I could go back in time, I would never let you leave…

HOLDING YOUR HAND

I held your hand for love.

I held your hand for security.

I held your hand to heal me.

I held your hand to help you.

I held your hand for the warmth I always craved.

I held your hand to guide me.

I held your hand to feel safe.

I held your hand for love...

NEVER FORGET

I can never forget the goodness of your soul.

I can never forget the selflessness you practiced daily.

I can never forget that smile that always warmed my heart and lit up these now-darkened hallways.

I can never forget the immense gratitude you felt every day.

I can never forget the tiny, simple things you did for me every day.

I can never forget your unrelenting courage in the face of the storms you bravely navigated.

I can never forget the absolute blessing that you were and are to me.

I can never, never forget...

YOUR SMILE

Your smile lit up a thousand rooms, your laugh echoed through miles of mountains.

Your selflessness has lovingly wrapped around hundreds of people.

Your intense love for me gave me the safest of havens.

I am so blessed to have been your life partner for thirty years.

I spend each day now looking into the spirit you left behind; a spirit that warms every corner of this home and reminds me of the blessing that was you.

FINDING YOU

I am trying to find myself in the empty rooms filled with your absence.

Wherever I look, I see your fingerprints on the fabric of my heart.

You are everywhere and nowhere.

You are elusive yet nearby.

You are the shadow I am running toward but landing in empty sadness.

You are the jar I want to fill with hope.

You are everything and nothing.

You are everywhere and nowhere,

I miss your spirit, your laughter, your contagious smile, and your positive soul.

I miss you.

I miss us.

I will never be the same without you.

THE EPIPHANIES OF GRIEF

Being in a fugue is my protective state.

A desire to move forward because it is too painful to stay in this depressive lacuna your death created.

The uncomfortable clarity of my circumstance and a stark contrast of my life now.

I can be okay for a while; I cannot be okay all day.

I learned that when forced to, I can manage this home of ours after all.

I learned I can be too busy and not provide myself with the necessary moments to grieve.

I learned that people are reticent to ask me how I am because it is too uncomfortable when I tell them the truth.

I learned that I must do the hard grief work if I have any desire to move not on, but forward and take with me the gift of our many memories.

I learned that I am strong, yet broken, half not whole, complete in my incompleteness, and consistent in my anxiety and fears.

I learned that when the small stinging bubbles of the waves of an ambush make themselves tangible, I must be ready to do the arduous work of grieving and healing from this assault on my life.

I learned that I have to go through this because I loved.

THINGS I MISS MOST ABOUT YOU

I miss your positive attitude every day no matter what challenges we had to face.

I miss your large and unlimited capacity to love.

I miss your solid integrity.

I miss that mega smile of yours that warmed my heart every day.

I miss your selflessness--the best of your numerous perfect characteristics.

I miss your willingness to take on pain yourself rather than imagine me suffering.

I miss your patience with everything.

I miss your kindness toward everyone you know and even just met.

I miss your charming ability to engage others to talk about themselves.

I miss the exacting care you took to provide a safe place for anyone to share their insecurities with you, and your uncanny way of reassuring them through love and acceptance.

I miss that wink of yours that reminded me that you loved me.

I miss your sometimes raucous laughter that boomed and echoed through the house.

I miss your romanticism.

I miss your asking me to renew our wedding vows.

I miss how you never let things bother you, even the major things.

I miss your sterling character, which you absolutely would not compromise for anyone or anything.

I miss how deeply and fearlessly you loved me.

THE WIDOWS CLUB

You do not belong in this club if you have not experienced the bone-crushing embrace of the grief of losing your spouse.

You do not belong to this club if any viable tissue in your heart has not been damaged for good.

You do not belong to this club if your breathing does not become inexplicably labored just at the very thought of your loss.

You do not belong to this club if your stomach does not tighten in the grip of pain when you hear a familiar love song.

You do not belong to this club if you are not sleeping on only one side of the bed because it is too painful to pull down the covers on the other side.

You do not belong to this club if you walk around the now mausoleum-like hollow of your house and do not hear the echoes of a voice that once passed through these halls.

You do not belong to this club if every light in the house is not turned on in an eternal vigil for the one gone.

You do not belong to this club if you do not need all the power you can muster to get out of the grips of the bed that was once the safest of havens.

You do not belong to this club if you are not aimlessly and mindlessly pursuing any semblance of your new identity everywhere you go.

You do not belong to this club if your life has not been precisely razor-sliced in half with the devastating and abrupt absence of the one that made sense of your life.

You do not belong to this club if you do not agonize over the simple things that have no value in their ability to distract you from this nightmare of your loss.

You do not belong to this club if you are not torn away from what you thought was an inextricably strong suture that would hold you together forever.

You should be so grateful if you do not belong to this club. I never wanted a membership.

A NEW YEAR WITHOUT YOU

I am feeling…

A sense of loss that is so profound that it weighs me down despite any effort on my part to ignore it or move forward to something else.

A separation that tragically tears my spirit and body apart, leaving the ragged raw edges of my unrepairable heart profusely bleeding in its attempt to beat.

A feeling of purposelessness that I cannot wrap my arms or mind around.

The difficulty of managing to get out of bed on the newly damaged morning without a reason or a purpose to do so.

How hard it is to wake up at all to the absence of him who was my entire world.

The challenge of filling my already void days with mundane activities that unsuccessfully attempt to distract me from my distress.

Fear of what my future holds, and how I will navigate the narrow and perilous roads alone into the final act of my life.

Sadness for what we would have shared in the years ahead that has now traumatically ghosted me.

Overwhelming gratitude for the thirty years we had together, how we loved fiercely, how we supported each other, how selfless you were.

FINDING STRENGTH

I find strength in every now painfully healing thought of you.

I find strength in the soft memories of a perfectly imperfect love we shared.

I find strength in every corner of this home that is a manifestation of our love.

I find strength in the parting stone of your physical being that I lovingly hold in the palm of my eager hand every night that uninvitedly replaced your hand.

I find strength when I think of how blessed I am to have been the object of your desire for thirty joyful and loving years.

I find strength in the courage you instilled in me to move into the "I am" statement of my life.

I find strength in the faith you so resolutely expressed every day of your life.

I find strength in your last "I love you," which evaporated into a perpetual memory of our love and commitment to each other for so long.

I find strength in the validation you always unreservedly gave to me every day of my life with you.

I find strength in knowledge, unwavering faith, and illuminating hope that keeps me moving closer toward you in these days of the remainder of my life.

I find strength in everything you were and are to me in life and unwelcome death.

I find your strength in my unwanted life without you that keeps me going forward.

LESSONS OF LOVE

I learned how to care about others above myself.

I learned how to respect others even though I might not agree with them.

I learned to care for the ill.

I learned to live my life with integrity and humility.

I learned how suffering has brought me closer to God.

I learned how to love unconditionally.

I learned how to sacrifice my needs and desires to satisfy the needs of others.

I learned to serve and not be served.

I learned to speak truth to power with grace and eloquence.

I learned how to spend my life being grateful for even the smallest of blessings in all circumstances.

I learned how to turn anxiety into peacefulness.

I learned how to be patient and kind to everyone.

I learned how to deal with the imperfections of my body.

I learned how to trust in God and put my faith in the truth and everything He uses for good.

I learned how to make people feel significant and special.

I learned to dismiss the things that upset me as blockades to my peace of mind.

I learned to interpret feelings and be sensitive to the troubles of others.

I learned to forgive and let go totally.

I learned how to enjoy nature whether harsh weather or good.

I learned to tend a garden full of God's miracles.

I learned how to give second chances because we all need redemption.

I am learning how to move forward and continue your legacy of selflessness, caring, and compassion.

All of this I learned from you, your favored student in your class "Love 101."

INSPIRATION

You inspired me every day to be a better person with your exemplary abundant love.

You inspired me to see what is in someone's heart and reach out to them with comfort and compassion.

You inspired me to seize each day being grateful to the God who allowed me to breathe at its miraculous inception.

You inspired me to be selfless, knowing I could never measure up to the one who was the epitome of that characteristic.

You inspired me to write, to be raw with my story, and uninhibited in its release.

You inspired me to be patient because you always were with everything you encountered that should have been an obstacle.

You inspired me to pray, strengthen my faith, and not fear what comes next.

You inspired me by your example to find joy in my life and the beautiful simple things, as you continually bestowed your kindness and unrelenting love upon me.

You inspired me when you would be in awe of my stamina and my dedication to being my healthiest self.

You inspired me to accept things that do not always go my way.

You inspired me to forgive—a character trait you must have invented.

You inspired me through your death to reach for a new purpose, to continue your legacy of love and acceptance, and to move forward and walk proudly in the shadow of your strength.

You inspired me every day of our thirty years together.

I CHOSE A MAN WHO…

I chose a man who was committed to our covenant of abiding love.

I chose a man who was never threatened by any accomplishment he promoted in me.

I chose a man whose selfless living allowed me to blossom under that umbrella of love.

I chose a man who meant the world to me.

I chose a man of such honor and integrity.

I chose a man who lit up the world with God's love.

I chose a man with immense gratitude for the blessings and mercies of each day.

MY HOPE

My hope is that the memories of you never fade into a vaporous blur as time goes on without you.

My hope is that your smile, which illuminated my world and the world of so many others, never dims. Not even a little bit.

My hope is that I will carry your loving and selfless spirit deep within the fabric of my heart like a permanent and beautiful living tattoo.

My hope is that whatever I do, and wherever I go, thoughts of you never become ethereal, but become an imprint within the ventricles of my brain, secured into my permanent memory.

My hope is that I can someday, somehow carry on your enormous legacy of love, selflessness, and acceptance, words which you lived by all your life.

My hope is that somehow my tears of grief so frequently and unabashedly become a catalyst for healing and experiencing immense joy at just the thought of you instead of such sadness in your absence.

My hope is that the remarkable characteristics you have lived by-- compassion, caring, empathy, and love for everyone you touched during the precious years of your life will be the lasting and endurable tapestry on the canvas of

the lives of our children and grandchildren, and they will live on in them forever.

My hope is that we will be together again in a realm of total joy and love revisited.

THE RING

This ring signifies a sacred covenant with you and before God.

Worn for thirty years as a circle of hopeful love forever.

I wonder if I should wear it still our covenant broken through a tragic blessing.

   - your life saved from the prison of your unresponsive body; a beautiful mind destroyed.

I wear it still on these days that follow, each one begging the question- why?

It feels like pretending to still be married, though I am socially labeled as not.

I decide to wear it every day as a stark reminder of our requited love all those years.

I wear it to honor that place on my finger where you placed it with profound promises.

I wear it to remind me every day that you were here and not a vaporous cloud.

I still wear it to encourage me to walk forward in your immeasurably gracious and loving footsteps.

I wear it still to give me the courage to go forward through the darkness of my life now, and into the light of a hopeful

future continuing your legacy of love and unparalleled kindness.

I wear it now to remind me that there will be no cessation of grieving you, but only the memories of the depth of our commitment and unending love.

I wear it because it represents a beautiful and sacred interconnection of our souls, one still here and one in an unknown and mysterious realm.

I am wearing this ring because it is beautiful.

THANKING YOU FOR...

Loving me.

Choosing me to be your life partner for thirty beautiful and blessed years

Being my best supporter and cheerleader in every pursuit

Always being so proud of me

Being a gentleman always in every situation

Being patient with me and all my peculiarities

The million trivial things you did for me every single day

Never being afraid to cry

Pushing me to do the difficult things

Protecting me in every viable way

Allowing me to be who I am and loving me anyway

Letting me vent when I needed to even if what I said hurt you

Being a Christ follower all your life and into mine

Being a beacon of light to all the lives you touched

Taking care of me when I was sick

Taking care of our children whenever they needed you

Being the best Papaw of all Papaws on this earth

Taking care of the house and making it a haven for us

Always being attentive to my needs to a fault

Believing I am beautiful

Believing in me and always telling me I am intelligent and capable

Always involving me in your daily life and issues no matter how minuscule or mundane
Letting me help you through your many illnesses
Being the most selfless husband, father, and grandfather
Simply being you, the man I love still though a demise that has separated us into two distant realms

HOW AM I REALLY?

I have not been good. I have been lonely not for company, but for you. Thirty years of sharing what was deepest in meaning to us alone is gone in the veritable blink of an eye. I still struggle to believe and understand that this is where I am now, who I am now, and that the better half of me is gone.

I hope you heard every word I said to you on that fateful day even amid the disturbing and loud cacophony of heart monitor beeps charting your progress to the unknown, and the simulated ventilator breaths that were devoid of your natural breaths. I wish I had said those things a million times just as you did to me.

Every day I had affirmations of your love for me. Every day I had constant and consistent reminders of the depth of your love and the level to which you selflessly devoted yourself to me.

I am devastated over losing you. I am in astounding disbelief that you are no longer here. I am alone and sad most days. It has been eight months since you quietly passed from this realm to a mystical realm we know not of. I spend my days doing mundane things to distract me from your perplexing absence. The rooms in this house echo your voice and shadow your physical presence. Sometimes it is not easy to be in this house where all your love for us as a couple and family is prominently displayed within every inch of breathable space.

I am trying to grieve graciously. And it is getting increasingly more challenging. It is hard to sleep at night and harder to stay asleep knowing I will be waking up to this nightmare and not from it. It is hard for me to walk down the hallowed hallways of my past with you into darkness where you are nowhere to be found. I want you back.

THE PIANO KEYS

Today I read about black and white notes on the piano.

How each one delivers a different sound-a different tone.

Black discouraging and attempting to subvert our delicate state of emotions.

White encourages us to see how amazing life can be and the possibility of remarkable things.

We do not just live our lives in the tones of one or the other, but what they create together…a perfect harmonious state where each plays a significant lesson in our lives that is value-added.

I was the flat and sharps keys of our life, and you were the illuminating white keys creating such a perfect musical morphing of the two sounds that sought to meld together and create a beautiful musical tapestry of our lives together.

The blacks and whites were the significant ups and downs of our thirty years together.

Those disturbing black notes of adversity drew us closer and bound our heartstrings into an intricate web of commitment and dedication to our goals as a family.

The white notes- the cream on the cake of life with you.

And so, the music of my life now without you is devoid of that perfect harmony, muted so as not to remind me of the

melodies we danced to, loved through, celebrated with, and lived with inimitable joy.

My song is silent now. There is no emission of notes, black or white- just the silence of the music we once danced to.

PARADISE REVISITED

You are always surrounding me, yet unattainable. An all-consuming void I keep reaching into.

The hollow echo of your words I hear every day.

As I sit on this beautiful patio of life where all you planted has effloresced in a tapestry of royal and majestic colors, I am acutely aware of the irony of my reality.

What you planted to please me, I am reluctantly enjoying alone without its author.

Sitting in this paradisaic venue, which now belongs to only me, I am forced to think about the many things for which I am grateful.

What your loss has taught me has become the valuable, inextricable rhythm of my life now.

Sometimes asynchronous and disconcerting; other times hauntingly profound and somewhat hopeful.

The greatest and most challenging lesson is my unmitigated acceptance of the reality I refuse to see.

I look into the eyes of your picture and find within me a deep yearning for them to see me now. For me to see your bright eyes without the perpetual veil of what separates us clouding my vision.

I look at the smile on the face of your picture and the stark, fierce reality of never being its recipient again haunts me, shakes me up, spits me out, and leaves the indelible taste of overwhelming sadness in my heart.

Acceptance has been a persistent reminder that you will never be with me again in this ephemeral realm.

As I struggle through the challenge of accepting my loss, I have come to realize that I never knew the profound power of the three words of your Modis operandi; "acknowledgement, understanding, and acceptance." Words you thought I wearied of your constant speaking have now become the words I esteem, my mantra, my echo for a long time to be.

THE CAVE

I remember a dream I had many years ago. I walked into a dark cave. There was one candle lit that illuminated the cave and there was a large rocking chair. Someone was sitting on the chair. My curiosity peeked, I ventured further into the cave and what I saw was Jesus sitting on the chair, his piercing eyes upon me.

There was a very distinct feeling of warmth and safety, which felt as though it was encompassing me in a cocoon-like protection.

Things are dark in a cave, scary, and terrible things happen in a cave. My grief journey has repelled me into a dark cave of uncertainty and fear unlike anything before, even my lung cancer diagnosis.

I have never experienced this level of uncertainty and flailing. I think my early dream of seeing Jesus in that dark cave sitting in perfect peace and contentment gave me a type of quiet that is acutely calming and comforting.

I imagine Jesus in a dark and dangerous place, and, yet such peace and calm which seems grossly counterintuitive.

I am in this grief cave where painful images of your death haunt me causing me to confront my reality.

In this cave, I am reliving every painful day from your stroke to your sudden death.

In this cave, I am imagining what you must have felt or not been aware of because of your incapacities.

In this cave, I am desperately trying to reconcile any disturbing behaviors on my part through our thirty years together.

In this cave, I am pondering with powerful negativity and regrets I can glean- things I failed to do, to say, to show you.

In this cave, I am all about myself and the sheer terror of living alone without you.

In this dark cave, there is a disturbing inconsistency, and ever-changing shadows on the walls that distort reality, my stability. Yet, my dream remains prominent and seared into the membranes of my brain.

Jesus is there in this cave, waiting quietly for me to approach the Throne of Grace.

He is there in this cave to protect and comfort me, to mend my broken heart and crushed spirit.

I will sit steadfastly at the feet of His mighty rocking chair and quietly await my recovery.

THE CHOREOGRAPHY OF GRIEF

Grief is a complicated sequence of steps and movements through a time of unique challenges emotionally, mentally, physically, and spiritually.

A time when the ambushes of great loss threaten to thwart the spiritual journey seeking a glimmer of hope in the ethereal distance.

Grief is a pas de deux of the main dancers, sorrow, and truth, moving asynchronously into a deep fog where the threat of stumbling blocks halts the momentum of progress.

A difficult convoluted mosaic of challenging steps incapable of being mastered.

The steps in this dance of grief may painfully wax and wane.

The only thing to do is learn new steps every day through this now inimitable dance of life.

IMAGINING

Some days the glimmer of hope that is embedded in the tears of my grief manifests itself in the form of a kind of presence—a white butterfly flitting in and out of my reality, the bright flight of a red Cardinal, a soft breeze through the trees of my own reverie.

I can let myself begin to believe that I can be okay without you.

It is then that I can imagine you sitting in the majestic, bucolic, inexpressible gardens of Heaven, wondering why you thought our earthly garden so grand.

I can imagine that the music you loved so much here on earth is just a cacophony of unrelatable discordant notes compared to the ineffable and haunting music of Heaven leaving you speechless.

I can imagine the mosaic of evocative and exotic colors of Heaven are startling to you leaving the colors of your human life on earth so somber as to diminish their impact entirely.

I can imagine in this perfect, glorious place, your soul set free with the release of all your physical pain gone, never to debilitate you again.

I can imagine the joy of your soul celebrating with our loved ones who have gone before us.

I can imagine you are at your highest, most heavenly achievable level of joy sitting at the feet of the Throne of Grace talking with God, knowing now all the answers to any questions you may have entertained on earth.

I can imagine this mystical realm that you now inhabit is far greater than anything we had here together.

In my imagining, is joy for you.

In my imagining, is an enfeebling sadness I am without you for the remainder of my days.

In my imagining, I will be with you again in that mystical realm of far-surpassing beauty, extraordinary love, and living grace.

All at once the glimmer of hope embedded in the tears of my grief starts to diminish, creating, again, a sadness so unappealing and so remote from where you are without me.

The burden of keeping your memories afloat while I am drowning in my new reality is a heavy one that I will never stop paddling to perpetuate.

MY LOSS

My loss has shredded my heart leaving ragged fragments of irregular sharp-edged pieces that will not ever fit together again.

My loss has broken my spirit, leaving me a permanent tortured soul searching for my purpose in life.

My loss has physically disabled me to the point of sheer unadulterated weariness.

My loss has rendered me helpless, making me lose all the logical perspective concerning my place in this life without you.

My loss has made me realize that the magical trip filled with immense love and joy for thirty years ended in a cascade of tragic events that released your physical body into the spiritual realm of the utmost joy.

My loss is unbearable at times and at other more subtle times, has taught me acceptance in the most brutal way- a reluctant acceptance that is perpetually residing in my head and heart.

My loss has left me hopelessly hopeful and at times rearing its ugly facade of incessant loneliness.

My loss has also raised me up to trust in God increasingly each day because of its existence now in my life, and to put my faith in His words of compassion, mercy, and love.

My loss gives me, at times, a different visage of how the deep lacuna in the shape of you that is now inside my heart can be at least partially filled by walking forward simultaneously in your elusive footsteps while following God's light on the path at my feet.

THE MUSCLE MEMORY OF GRIEF

In the movie, "Good Grief," the main character, who has lost a loved one, is speaking to an attorney about how when we love someone our brain imprints that person in our memory, and it is constantly mapping out seeking to find that person.

Like muscle memory, the fibers of our being are consistently piecing together the logic of the existence and now absence of that loved one in our life.

When that person, that loved one, dies, muscle memory continues to futilely track down their presence in our life and inevitably evolve into cells of Zen tangled unrecognizable patterns of disorientation.

Our brains are seeking to make sense of a catastrophic tearing away of the host of vital cells that belonged to that lost person- half of us now forever gone. The mapping is trying to halt its unrealistic progress.

The memory ripped away from the mainframe of our brain. The situation creates chaos in our heads and irreparable damage to the fabric of our minds and hearts.

Every day I am experiencing the illogical Zen tangle of my grieving and peripatetic brain waves.

The incongruency I experience cannot ever be reconciled in my mind and broken heart.

STEADFAST

You remained steadfast through all the trials in your life.

You never complained.

You withstood the pain whether physical or emotional.

Your faith was your fortress that protected you and gave you the unparalleled strength to keep moving forward.

You elucidated gratitude for your life as it was.

Steadfastness under trials promised you the Crown of Life.

I am sure God greeted you as a good and faithful servant as you passed silently from this realm to one we know little about.

An imperfect man who was made glorious by the life you led and the legacy you left behind.

I am now left wondering how God's expectations of me will manifest in my life of grief.

How do I remain steadfast in my journey without you?

How do I redefine myself in God's eyes?

Will God show me who I am amid my circumstances?

I am utterly lost; I am at a loss. I have lost so much of myself in your death that I am not anyone right now.

I am the lost sheep,

I am waiting on God to re-identify me- to help me re-identify myself.

There is nothing so sad or poignant as being lost within God's grasp and that is where I am without you.

LOSE TO GAIN

I had to lose you to reconcile and surrender to God.
I had to lose you to learn how to keep moving forward to an uncertain future without you.
I had to lose you to realize the impact you had on me for thirty beautiful years.
I had to lose you to grow in strength and formidable courage.
I had to lose you to conscientiously consider everything I must be grateful for.
I had to lose you to find my shattered self in a forest fire of grief.
I had to lose you to glean a certain knowledge of my place in my life.
I had to lose you with unspeakable sadness to realize the influence you had on me and still do.
I had to lose you to get on my knees and alert a God who attempts to paint the colors of love on the canvas of my soul.
I had to lose you to learn how to take care of myself and this home without guidance from you.
I had to lose you to gain the ability to accept the circumstance of my inevitable perpetual loneliness.
I had to lose you to realize that I am a capable person who was locked in your protective custody for so long.
I had to lose you to begin the tortuous journey of finding who I am without you.
I had to lose you to fully surrender on my knees to a God who, I am sure, hears my piteous laments.

I had to lose you to keep stepping into the stark realization of my situation and its interminable incapacitating sequela with gratitude and grace.
I had to lose you to find a singular vestige- a glimmer of hope for my new undesired future.
I had to lose you to begin navigating the muscle memory of my brain that futilely maps your ephemeral existence incessantly.
I had to lose you to come to an understanding that God takes what is His regardless of my forlorn groanings.
I had to lose you to gain a greater, more comprehensive spirituality in my relationship with God.
I had to lose you to realize just what you meant to me in the wake of the mundane world in which we live.

THE RECOVERY BREATH

This is not the way it was supposed to be- me here and you now are perpetually absent.

It is so difficult to fathom the remainder of my life without you.

We were supposed to grow older than we were together for many years.

Yet here I am alone to serve out the remainder of my years.

I am reduced to being a godforsaken word, "widow" rambling on about what I have lost.

Your death does not make sense in my logical world.

Medically, it is a wonder you survived the indignities of your many illnesses to come out on the other side.

But this time the indignity was a tremendous burden, which you could not bear for exceptionally long. Those illnesses took you away.

Charles Spurgeon says it, that the" Lord gets his best soldiers in the highlands of affliction."

I do not feel like a strong soldier amid the affliction of losing you. More a lonely and weak guard trying to protect my asynchronously beating heart, which has shattered into a million pieces, none of which is recoverable.

I am grieving for you who were my entire world, who meant everything to me.

Grieving for my yesterdays with you and fighting against the commencement of my future days alone.

I am flailing in an ocean with terrifyingly huge waves that overpower and threaten my very existence.

I am rising, falling, and rising again attempting to catch a recovery breath after fighting so hard to swim away from it all.

Nighttime falls and the stars that stubbornly continue to twinkle in your absence still attempt to illuminate the darkened corners of my forlorn soul.

Stars that, unbelievably, create a slight glimmer of light barely visible yet discernibly still defiantly there.

THE ODYSSEY OF GRIEF

Traversing the torturous road of grief-

  the most challenging to navigate.

There is no bypass to avoid the busyness of dark thoughts and the brutal clangs of your absence.

No exit signs to veer off this unnegotiable road.

No pleasant lookouts to distract.

  only the solemness of the rough road crown.

Pebbles of grief flying into my heart.

Destroying, tearing, dismantling an already insulted organ.

The topology created unrecognizable, uninhabitable.

The distant horizon seen through a narrowing peripheral vision slowly claiming the land of my mortality.

The absence of you- the horizon ever fading away

  unable to be visualized no matter the try.

THE PIECES OF MY PUZZLE

The puzzle of my life once conformed to a magical tapestry of joy and love.

Creating a safe and secure prototype, the future of which was seemingly immovable and fixed.

Now abruptly scattered into a million pieces through a tragic loss caustically imposed.

Trying to reconstruct what was utterly disordered, leaving me searching for each vital piece in a pallid attempt to survive.

My logic claiming I cannot reorganize the intricate pieces of my now former life.

My heart begging God for the release from this defeat.

Little by little a semblance of reordering portending change.

Little by little each disrupted piece shoving itself into an imagined space no longer available or attainable.

The pieces floating around me in an ethereal nightmare, tempting me to pluck just one to begin to reconstruct the tapestry it once helped create.

My now much less-focused brain unable to choose which one to begin to put together a pathway moving toward a different hope.

THE CACAPHONY OF GRIEF

The stark absence of a loved one renders the most discordant noise in broken hearts and crushed spirits.

That absence is magnified through everything we ever experienced with the one we loved so deeply and fiercely.

Sounds that keep playing in hearts and minds like unrelenting earworms of looped memories.

Unable to be stopped, unable to be reconciled with.

Sounds that consistently and most persistently demand our reticent attention.

It is the sound of the horror of the absence of the half of you that has been torn away leaving the most irritating and raw, unrepairable edges in the chambers of my heart.

I am mourning the loss of me and not the loss of a great man I loved for so long.

The sounds he is hearing now in that mystical, unexplainable realm are the magical notes of the highest order of the very intricate music we will never hear in this realm.

I must continue to listen to the warbled, discordant, unrelatable notes of my grief.

I must be thankful that he can never hear that discordance again, only the magnificent, unfathomable notes of the heart of God.

Those notes of eternal bliss He placed within our innermost being to be manifested only for His glory.

THE WHITE BUTTERFLY

From the first dim light of dawn, dare I believe your persistent presence is a reminder of your watchful soul?

You flit in and out everywhere I am- around the bloodless vessels of my broken heart.

Are you trying to find a way back to fill the hole your absence tragically created?

Or are you just symbolic of my peripatetic mind weaving in and out of logic, still trying to find you somewhere, anywhere.

The healing of my irretractable brokenness, the ephemeral notion of purity and peace try to punctuate a hope I have yet to comprehend.

I am waiting patiently for the mysterious transformation you portend.

I am desperately seeking the fleeting connection I must now make with the spiritual entity you portray.

Wanting a renewal of my psyche- a new beginning toward the exodus of this debilitating grief.

The lonely journey has begun and is arduously integrating with the quotidian of my every day.

The radiance of your wings reflects a transient glimmer of healing and hope- a renewed hope,

And it lights my path to eventual evolvement.

MY PRAYER

For what do I pray as my loneliness and grief-stricken soul become magnified stronger each day without you?

Do I pray for a returned state of wholeness while half of me is still gone forever?

Shall I pray for a new purpose-the last one sadly dissipating into an ethereal bubble floating away so far from me.

Is there any hope that my prayer will lessen the pain in this tortured grieving soul today, or the loneliness that tries to befriend me daily wanting to hold a hand I cannot offer?

Will praying stop the incessant tears that flow or prevent grief from taking up permanent residence in my fractured heart?

Do I pray for the realignment of the dislocated pieces of me and how do I approach the Throne of Grace with my persistent cries for a love loss?

I am practicing the practice of prayer each day in the hopes of a glimmer of light at the end of this suffocating, dark tunnel.

I am not begging God for a return of who cannot be returned, but rather a quiet release from the indelible pain of the tattoo of grief imprinted on my heart.

I am praying for the process of repair to my injured vessels that hemorrhage uncontrollably desperately seeking an even partial stasis.

My prayer is a mere plea for a way to find the half of me who is gone in the me who remains without.

A RESIGNED ACCEPTANCE

No one belongs to me, not even you.

I loved you wholly but learned through your death that I held you too tight.

I needed to delicately release the stronghold- to let you go because you did not belong to me.

You were purely lent to me through grace and mercy- to give a purpose higher than myself.

You were bestowed from God, so you were never really mine, though my wanting heart claimed every part of your soul.

The gift of you graced my life with blessings abounding every single day of our life together.

The depth of gratitude is too difficult to assess, a weight now heavy on my afflicted heart.

Acceptance comes at a risk of losing what I held most cherished – our covenant of love.

Acceptance wreaks havoc with my better angels, a pejorative blight on the tapestry of my heart.

It is the denial I repeatedly profess of that which I cannot accept.

Yet there- a pivotal flicker of hope brings me closer to the reality of which I despair, and the lessons of my acceptance are briefly elucidated.

Lessons of celebration of unparalleled love and joy at being the memory keeper of our lives together.

Lessons of hope for a better future than the one I now foresee.

Lessons of surrender to a trust in a God who will direct my path forward.

COMPASSIONATE CLARITY

Reflecting on my inner self, I can see areas of my life that are foreign to me.

The grace I try to extend myself, the paucity of which still inexplicable, is arduous to claim.

Compassionate clarity escapes my fractured heart and fails to put a mirror on my wounded soul.

Understanding where I am in this unenviable transition, compassion presents a challenge for my damaged heart.

As weeks and months pass into a year and true clarity begins its role, I am acutely in a state of shock and fear.

There is a hollowness in my already vacant soul that lucidity of mind has yet to fill.

A deep divide between logic and disjointed state.

I am forced to evolve yet suspended still in the median plane of true compassionate clarity.

THE MAGNIFYING GLASS

The magnification of my tortured soul resolutely resides in my inner being.

It transforms the picture of my fractured heart into unidentifiable pieces.

The magnification of my sorrowful state distorts every waking realm of my reality, leaving me to ponder a purpose I now cannot perceive.

The magnification of the grief I bear brings into sharpened focus a state of mind I know cannot be sustained.

The magnification of the depth of our love judged pure by sunlight is ever present and begs for a translucent view of the substance of our spent sacred covenant.

The magnification of our blessed and joy-filled years together, the hopes and dreams sliced short, give way to a gratitude long overdue.

The magnification of the lessons you taught overwhelmed my intellect and illuminated my vaguely hopeless heart.

The magnifying glass that elucidates lost blessings will in perpetuity be my light.

THE AURA OF US

When I imagine us as we used to be before God took you away from me,

I can feel the warmth surrounding us that many could discern.

There was something mystical between us that burst into rays of great love.

An aura transforming and traversing into a magical place of peace and joy.

Safety elucidated through a myriad of mindful words and acts.

That aura was my resting place where only we resided.

It formed our own impenetrable fortress and kept us reminded of how precious, how rare, how wholly present it was.

That aura now diffused--the visceral pain from which I cannot be released.

My maudlin heart and afflicted mind are still searching for you-pointlessly seeking you to no avail.

I still feel that aura surrounding me indigenous by design, though a year has passed since your demise leaving behind a fractured heart- inevitably irreparable.

And my brain still maps you out though a futile journey it is, capturing only the diminishing and   otherworldly aura of you.

THE UNDERLYING TONE OF MY LIFE

The underlying tone of my life now is sadness, quiet despair, incessant fear of the future.

The underlying tone of my life speaks to a cruel realization of my loss.

It raises unanswerable questions of my purpose, who I am, the why's and the what if's.

The underlying tone of my life tries to prepare me for a future of things lost, memories fading, and a shattered and fractured heart painfully trying to heal.

The underlying tone of my life reveals suffering defined, but not acceptable as such.

The underlying tone of my life seeks redemption from the overwhelming and relentless grief.

The underlying tone of my life struggles daily to find a glimmer of hope, a ray of light indicative of thriving.

THE VEINS OF MY GRIEF

There is a deep and immobilizing sorrow coursing through the veins of my grief, lingering at the back flow of its valves.

Attempting to prevent a necessary supply of the liquid lifeline back to my fractured and irreparable heart.

It resides in me no matter the transient joyful moments and attempts to restrain the scarcity of hope in my nebulous attempt to move forward.

This sorrow inhabits the shape of love lost forever and attempts to blur beautiful memories and the imagination of opportunities now lost.

It desperately embraces this unwilling recipient claiming an unavailable territory of my heartland that is the embodiment of lost love.

Its cruel attempts to sabotage my sporadic joy now met with the least resistance- its power too difficult to thwart.

I am struggling to fathom a life without you, and I am now forced to confront this veil of perpetual loneliness and dismiss any direction toward a light, dim as it may now be.

At times, these veins of my grief throb with the impulses of a sanguine renewal lending a ray of expectation, lighting the path upon which I am now a hopeful sojourner.

YOU WROTE MY STORY

A million little things connect the fragile threads of my life.

The insignificant cast aside into fading remnants of pallidness.

The significant rise from the erosion of those faded to form a majestic mosaic of experiences in my life with you.

These experiences call me every day in their attempt to either sabotage or enlighten me—to remind me of what I lost.

My story was sculpted out with the promise we gave each other, and the life lessons you taught me in our poignant odyssey.

My story became an aggregate of your unfailing protection, your fierce love, your deep dedication no matter discord or harmony, your unfailing faithfulness, and your trust.

My story began with the thoughtful things you did, the myriads of burdens from which I was spared.

My story began with the touch of your hands that comforted and calmed me—your smile that lit up the chambers of my heart.

My story strengthened in its hold over the love I had for you, becoming a tether to your goodness.

Everything you said and did engraved a permanent indelible sentence on the pages of my life book.

It became an imbued tattoo stitched to the fabric of my now exsanguinated heart.

My story began with your heartbeat next to mine, steady and strong.

My story ended with the discordant, palpably enfeebled agonal rhythm of your demise.

Time for Hope

THE LADY OF THE WOODS

A little wooden heart engraved with your spirit; I hang on the white branch of the tree of renewal and rebirth.

The clarity of its presence seen in the autumn of my life without you.

A visible symbol of protection and survival amid the quagmire of my grief is seen in the sparkles of a hope I had feared never to attain.

The silvery white branch of this beautiful birch – a stark contrast to the dark and broken heart I protectively shield.

As winter sets in, no leaf to be found adorning the branches, the enhanced reality of a lost soul even now instills a glimmer of reasonable hope, yet distant from reach.

A hope portending a strong willingness to exist and grow.

A hope of new beginnings still carrying the essence of your spirit in my psyche.

A deeply rooted hope transcending moments of sorrow so overtly displayed.

A hope for purification of the bereavement that has tortured my fractured soul.

A hope to nullify the harsh dissonance in the asynchronous beating of my heart.

Clothed with this new hope, I see the beauty that spring's revival brings and the summer's warmth that sustains.

As winter sets in with the promise of spring, I am ready and anxious to see your heart again on the blessed branch of the Lady of the Woods.

Acknowledgements

My deepest gratitude for my children whose unconditional love, support, and encouragement during my darkest time of grief and all through my life, who remind me every day that I am not alone, and I am dearly loved.

I feel immense gratitude for my extended family for always being in support mode and loving me through all the difficult and not so difficult times in my life.

I am thankful for my dear and amazing friends from all aspects of my life, professional and personal, who have touched my life and left a positive imprint on the fabric of my soul.

A special thanks to my Pastor, David Smith, from Fairhaven Church in Centerville, Ohio, who is always there when I need to talk and whose support is a healing jewel in the painful process of my grieving.

I am forever grateful to my editor and publisher, Rebecca Benston, of Higher Ground Books & Media, who believed in the value of my writing not once, but twice, and for having the confidence that my words will somehow help others through the grieving process.

I am deeply grateful to God for giving me my late husband, Ron Coleman, who for thirty years loved me, cherished me, believed in me, inspired me, took intense care of me and taught me so many precious life lessons, and who continues to send me ethereal signs of love and validation for everything I now do in this realm.

I continue to be grateful to my dear friend and mentor of twenty-three years, Dr. William Felker, who taught me the value of writing from my heart.

I am hopeful that anyone who is going through the painful process of grieving a loved one may discover delicate morsels of hope and gratitude through my poetry of grief.

Other titles from Higher Ground Books & Media:
One Day in May by Joanne Piccari Coleman
Finding Purpose in the Pain by Brenda W. McIntyre
The Story I Tell by Rebecca Whited
Meant to Be by Becka L. Jones
From Judgment to Jubilee by Rebecca Benston
Shine Like Stars by Rev. Jerry C. Crossley
Shameless Persistence by Sandra Bretting
God's Whispers by Christine Nekas-Thoma
Raven Transcending Fear by Terri Kozlowski
The Frost of Lost Words by Stephen Shepherd
Journey to the Mountaintop by Terra Kern
Healing in God's Power by Yvonne Green
The Real Prison Diaries by Judy Frisby
The Bottom of This by Tramaine Hannah
My Name is Sam by Joe Siccardi

Add these titles to your collection today!
http://www.highergroundbooksandmedia.com

HIGHER GROUND BOOKS & MEDIA IS

AN INDEPENDENT PUBLISHER

Do you have a story to tell?

Higher Ground Books & Media is an independent Christian-based publisher specializing in stories of triumph! Our purpose is to empower, inspire, and educate through the sharing of personal experiences. We are always looking for great, new stories to add to our collection. If you're looking for a publisher, get in touch with us today!

Please be sure to visit our website for our submission guidelines.

http://www.highergroundbooksandmedia.com/submission-guidelines

HGBM SERVICES IS OUR CONSULTING FIRM

AUTHOR SERVICES

HGBM Services offers a variety of writing and coaching services for aspiring authors! We can help with editing, manuscript critiques, self-publishing, and much more! Get in touch today to see how we can help you make your dream of becoming an author a reality!

*****

We also offer social media marketing services for authors, small businesses, and non-profit organizations. Let us help you get the word out about your book, your projects, and your mission. We offer great rates, quality promos, consistent communication, and a personal touch!

http://www.highergroundbooksandmedia.com/editing-writing-services

Need Bulk Copies?

If you would like to order bulk copies of this book or any other title at Higher Ground Books & Media, please contact us at highergroundbooksandmedia@gmail.com.

We offer discounts for purchases of 20 or more copies. Excellent for small groups, book clubs, classrooms, etc.

Get in touch today and get a set of great stories for your students or group members.

www.ingramcontent.com/pod-product-compliance
Lightning Source LLC
Chambersburg PA
CBHW060848050426
42453CB00008B/887